P9-ARA-592

HIDDEN ANIMAL COLORS

JANE PARK

◪ MILLBROOK PRESS / MINNEAPOLIS

Animals SHOW OFF spectacular colors—
PURPLE,
YELLOW,
RED,
and GREEN!

Gouldian finch

But LOOK CLOSER at some plainer ones.

We might have COLORS not easily seen.

Mallard duck

I learned how to survive when I was young.
To SCARE away predators . . .

I STICK OUT MY TONGUE!

A **BLUE-TONGUED SKINK** shows its brightly colored tongue, puffs up its body, and hisses to confuse and **STARTLE** a predator.

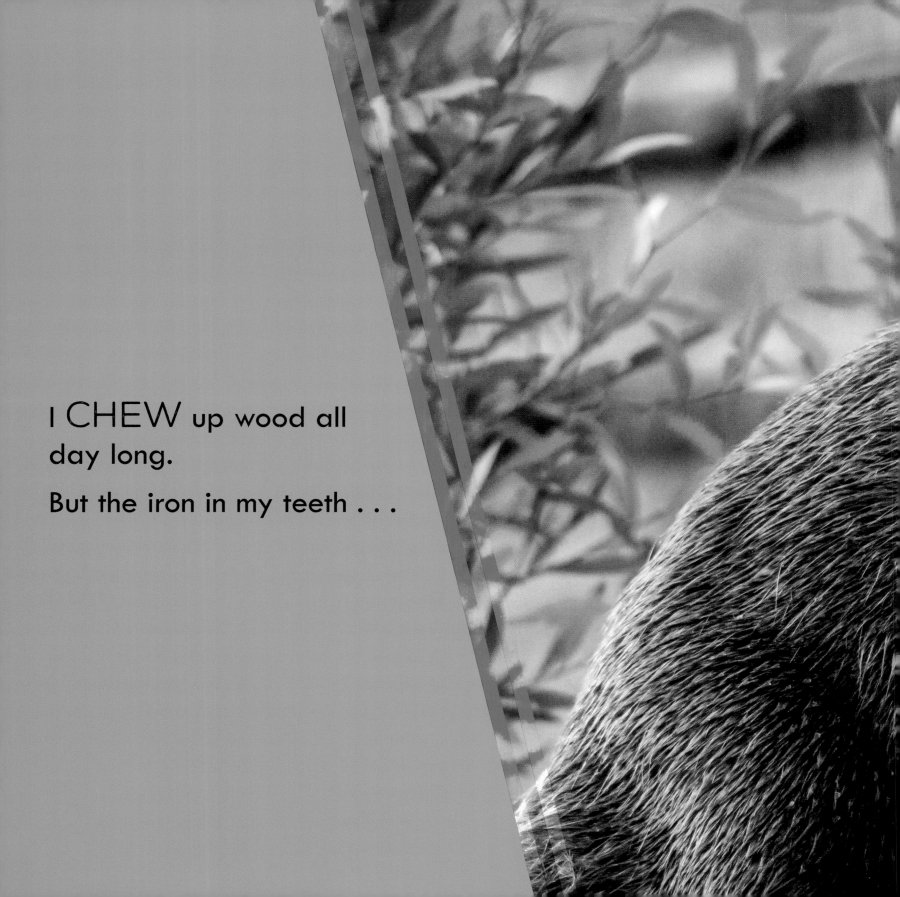

I CHEW up wood all day long.

But the iron in my teeth . . .

KEEPS THEM STRONG.

Iron makes a **BEAVER**'s teeth orange and as tough as can be! Beavers' teeth grow constantly, and they trim and sharpen their teeth when they gnaw on wood.

My FEATHERS may
be brown and ashy,

But the eggs that I lay . . .

ARE BRIGHT AND FLASHY.

The **TINAMOU**'s eggs might be **BRILLIANTLY** colored to attract other females to lay eggs in the same nest. Why? Predators often eat their eggs. But if the eggs are in a big pile together, a predator won't be able to eat them all.

I'm not as DULL as you might think.

To protect my skin . . .

I SWEAT PINK!

A **HIPPOPOTAMUS** makes its own special fluid to protect its skin. Although the fluid is not technically sweat, it has been called **BLOOD SWEAT** for its color. Hippos spend a lot of time in the sun and water. The fluid acts as a sunscreen, a water repellent, and a moisturizer.

My COLOR helps me stay out of sight.

But when I'm looking for a mate . . .

FAN-THROATED LIZARDS display their colorful dewlaps when they want attention. The females seem to prefer partners with more orange in their dewlaps. Orange might signal that the males are healthy, while blue and black may be linked to how **AGGRESSIVE** they are.

The iron in your BLOOD
makes it red.

But my blood has copper . . .

SO IT'S BLUE INSTEAD!

The copper in **HORSESHOE CRABS**' blood helps carry oxygen around their bodies, like the iron in our blood does. When copper meets oxygen, it often turns things **BLUE** or **GREEN**—like the Statue of Liberty.

My face is as
bright as autumn.

But my hidden
SURPRISE . . .

IS MY MATCHING BOTTOM!

The **MANDRILL** is one of the world's most colorful mammals. When a mandrill gets excited, its colors get even brighter!

The spots on my wings look like BIG owl eyes.
But watch for BRIGHT color . . .

WHEN I SPREAD MY WINGS AND FLY!

The **BLUE MORPHO BUTTERFLY** does not actually have blue pigment in its wings. We see the **STUNNING** color because of the way the tiny scales on the wings reflect light.

When we pay attention,
the ORDINARY can amaze us too.

Mallard duck

What else could we be missing?

Take a CLOSER look at what's around you!

CAN YOU GUESS THE REASONS FOR THE COLORATION OF THESE ANIMALS?

Color plays many different roles in the animal world. Animals may use colors to **attract** attention from partners. Or their colors may **startle and distract** predators. Some animals use **camouflage** to blend in and hide. And others use **mimicry** to look like a different, more threatening animal. Finally, coloration can be **incidental**—an animal's color is just because of the pigment in its blood or skin cells.

An animal can be a fit for more than one reason.

REASONS

A. Attraction

B. Camouflage

C. Mimicry

D. Distract or startle predators

E. Incidental

BEAVER

BLUE MORPHO BUTTERFLY

BLUE-TONGUED SKINK

FAN-THROATED LIZARD

HIPPOPOTAMUS

HORSESHOE CRAB

TINAMOU

GLOSSARY

aggressive: likely to attack or use force against another

bacteria: microscopic organisms that are found everywhere. Some bacteria are good for your body, while others can make you sick.

camouflage: an animal's color or pattern that blends in with its surroundings

dewlaps: loose flaps of skin that hang from the necks of some animals

incidental: happening as an unimportant or unplanned part of something else

mammal: a warm-blooded animal (such as a dog, bear, whale, or human being) that has a backbone and hair, and that feeds milk to its young

pigment: any color in plant or animal cells. Most cells contain pigment.

reflect: to throw back (waves of light, sound, or heat) without absorbing

secretion: a substance made and released by a living thing (like tears, snot, or sweat)

FURTHER READING

Books

Algarra, Alejandro. *Why Are Animals Different Colors?* Hauppauge, NY: Barron's Educational Series, 2016.

Lawler, Janet. *Rain Forest Colors*. Washington, DC: National Geographic Kids, 2014.

Neal, Christopher Silas. *Animal Colors*. Brooklyn, NY: Little Bee Books, 2018.

Salas, Laura Purdie. *Crayola® Wild World of Animal Colors*. Minneapolis: Lerner Publications, 2019.

Websites

American Museum of Natural History
What's This? Colorful Creatures
https://www.amnh.org/explore/ology/zoology/what-s-this-colorful-creatures

Arizona State University
Animal Colors That Catch the Eye
https://askabiologist.asu.edu/animal-colors-and-patterns

New Hampshire PBS
Deceptive Coloration
https://nhpbs.org/natureworks/nwep2a.htm

For Hannah, Owen, and Mia
and always, Ena the Echidna and Keo the Cone Snail

Millbrook Press™
An imprint of Lerner Publishing Group, Inc.
241 First Avenue North
Minneapolis, MN 55401 USA

For reading levels and more information, look up this title at www.lernerbooks.com.

Image credits: Simia Attentive/Shutterstock.com, p. 1; erperlstrom/Getty Images, p. 2; Jean Landry/Getty Images, p. 3; Andrew Hutchings/Shutterstock.com, pp. 4, 5, 6, 7, 30; Troy Harrison/Getty Images, pp. 8, 9; Robert McGouey/Wildlife/Alamy Stock Photo, pp. 10, 11, 30; John Holmes/Alamy Stock Photo, pp. 12, 13, 30; BIOSPHOTO/Alamy Stock Photo, p. 14; Radek Borovka/Shutterstock.com, p. 15; Winner/Alamy Stock Photo, pp. 16, 30; Eric Baccega/naturepl.com, p. 16; John Sullivan/Alamy Stock Photo, p. 17; HIRA PUNJABI/Alamy Stock Photo, pp. 18, 19, 30; David Santiago Garcia/Getty Images, pp. 20, 21, 30; Piotr Naskrecki/Minden Pictures, p. 22; Anup Shah/Getty Images, p. 23; mbrand85/Shutterstock.com, p. 24; Fotofeeling/Getty Images, p. 25; OGphoto/Getty Images, pp. 26, 27, 30; Reibertb/500px/Getty Images, pp. 28, 29; fivespots/Shutterstock.com, p. 32.
Cover image: Super Prin/Shutterstock.com.
Jacket: Super Prin/Shutterstock.com; fivespots/Shutterstock.com; W&AC Visual Arts/Getty Images.

Designed by Emily Harris.
Main body text set in Tw Cen MT Std.
Typeface provided by Monotype Typography.

Library of Congress Cataloging-in-Publication Data

Names: Park, Jane (Children book author), author.
Title: Hidden animal colors / Jane Park.
Description: Minneapolis : Millbrook Press, [2022] | Includes bibliographical references. | Audience: Ages 5–9 | Audience: Grades K–1 | Summary: "Nature is full of browns and grays. But some animals feature pinks, blues, aand greens. Brilliant photos accompany lyrical nonfiction text to explore animals' hidden colors" —Provided by publisher.
Identifiers: LCCN 2021014571 (print) | LCCN 2021014572 (ebook) | ISBN 9781728445663 (library binding) | ISBN 9781728445694 (ebook)
Subjects: LCSH: Animals—Color—Juvenile literature.
Classification: LCC QL767 .P245 2022 (print) | LCC QL767 (ebook) | DDC 591.47/2—dc23

LC record available at https://lccn.loc.gov/2021014571
LC ebook record available at https://lccn.loc.gov/2021014572

Manufactured in the United States of America
1-50263-49875-9/13/2021